Support for Alzheimer's and Dementia Caregivers:
The Unsung Heroes

Judith L. London, Ph.D.

2013

ISBN: 1482375915
ISBN-13: 9781482375916

Library of Congress Control Number: 2013908431
CreateSpace Independent Publishing Platform
North Charleston, South Carolina

Contents

PART II
ON THE HOMEFRONT: STIRRING THE OATMEAL

STORY:

PART III
STRESS: RELEASE VALVES

STORY:

PART IV
NEW DIRECTIONS: NO SIGNPOSTS

STORY:

PART V
HELP FOR UNSUNG HEROES

Acknowledgment

To:
Bob, Kathy, Chris, Janet,
Mary Claire, Amy, Pam and **Jan**,
And my Avenidas clan,
How you made this happen again.
Grateful am I to be so blessed
To have a team
That is THE BEST.

Introduction

Caregivers are unsung heroes. Yes, you who take care of someone in your family, or a friend, with Alzheimer's or another dementia, demonstrate how much that person means to you in a way that shows courage and sacrifice. It is heroic. And no one awards you a medal for the job you perform.

As I speak around the country about my first book, *Connecting the Dots: Breakthroughs in Communication as Alzheimer's Advances*, you, the professionals and the family caregivers, tell me that you long for relief, for some understanding as you travel this road. Written just for you - whether a newcomer or a seasoned caregiver - *Support for Alzheimer's and Dementia Caregivers: The Unsung Heroes* is a book that offers comfort and sustenance throughout this long journey.

As you have discovered, caregiving during the course of a disease that affects the brain goes far beyond the arduous task of taking care of someone who can directly express his needs during an illness. Often, people with Alzheimer's and other dementias are unable to let you know what they need in a direct manner. Taking care of someone's unspoken needs is frustrating, exhausting and overwhelming. You think: if only my mother could tell me what's wrong instead of screaming. If only my husband would stop pulling clothes out of the dresser. It would make my life so much easier.

And the sad thing is that the person would tell you - if he could. It falls upon you to deal with the mystery of garbled communication - of how to make sense of it all. You may feel upset, angry, or depressed. Throughout the process of caregiving, you grieve as you lose the way your loved one used to be. You grieve as you see how Alzheimer's has changed the way *you* used to be.

Inevitably, you neglect yourself, only to feel so filled with stress that you risk becoming emotionally and physically ill. You have plenty of company. In the United States alone, nearly 15 million of the unpaid caregivers like you give care at home for 80% of those with Alzheimer's. Reports indicate that among unpaid caregivers:

- 61% have very high emotional stress
- 43% have physical stress

Added to that are the millions more of unpaid caregivers who deal with other types of dementia, as well as paid caregivers, many of whom leave this work because of job stress and strain. [1]*

Who takes care of you? The preoccupation with someone else's needs echoes in your mind. You face the challenge of how to maintain your equilibrium as you deal with this illness. What an undertaking that is. Many of you hold full-time jobs in addition to an average of 22 hours a week you may spend caring for your loved one. Many of you have the full responsibilities of a spouse or parent, roles that are crucial to your whole family. Many of you return home after a hard day's work, not to rest, but to take care of others.

---

1 *Alzheimer's Association Report, 2013. Alzheimer's Disease Facts and Figures

Who has time for oneself when day and night evaporate so quickly? No wonder you feel overwhelmed.

Support for Alzheimer's and Dementia Caregivers: The Unsung Heroes is divided into five main parts:

- Changes: Lost and Found
- On the Home Front: Stirring the Oatmeal
- Stress: Release Valves
- New Directions: No Signposts
- Help for Unsung Heroes

Inspirational poems open all five parts of the book, and within each of the first four sections, you will find a series of stories with validating, nurturing messages that highlight each story. Each story, based on comments caregivers have shared with me and others, stands alone and can be read or re-read slowly, one at a time. You may feel that you are in a support group meeting when you read, *From One Extreme to Another...* or experience unexpected joy in *The Magic of Shakespeare*. You may find comfort in *Golf Anyone? Once You Get Him Started.* Throughout the book, you will notice that 'he' and 'she' are used alternately but the stories apply to either gender or whatever your role is in the caregiving process.

In Part V, Help for Unsung Heroes, you will see a summary of the highlights, definitions, and coping tips. For convenience, you will find a guide to dominant themes so you can easily find the stories that reflect how you feel today.

Husbands and wives, partners, daughters and daughters-in-law, sons and sons-in-law, grandchildren, other relatives, and paid professionals as well, all have much in common regardless of the person in their lives with this disease. Physicians, psychologists, social workers, activities therapists, R.N.s and nurses' aides: you are among those who rarely receive support for the laudable efforts and the work you do. This book is for you, too.

Caregivers need support to survive dementia diseases without becoming a casualty. We need each other to cope. All that you do, all that you give of yourselves, proclaims the news:

You are the unsung heroes.

PART I

Changes: Lost and Found

What have I lost?
I have lost the way you used to be.
In some ways, this is good, although
I cannot believe I just said that.
In other ways, most ways,
It is painful and
It makes me sad.

What have I found?
The new you,
Reminiscent of the old you. But different.
I have found
The new me,
One that is more resilient than I ever thought.
One that can still laugh, then cry,
One that is facing the
Unfaceable
With
Head held high.

Judith London 2012

STORY 1

What's Going On?

Every few days I call my 80-year-old mother at 12 noon to see how she is. Today, the phone rings on and on. She doesn't pick up. I start to worry. I decide to drop by to see if she's OK. I'm shocked at what I find.

"Mom, Mom!" I keep leaning on the doorbell with one finger and rapping on the door with my clenched left fist. I stop to comb through my purse, hoping to find that extra key to her house. My fingers close over the metal teeth, and I pull out the key, relieved. I insert it and feel thankful again that Mom only has this one dead bolt lock and not a chain as well. The latch clicks and I open the door.

"Mom? Mom? It's me, Julie, and I'm here. Where are you, Mom?"

I feel my face line with worry as I dash around the house. When I reach the dining room, I stop in my tracks. The table is filled with scattered papers, torn open envelopes, some on the floor. I close in on the mess, and see notices of sweepstakes and the 'you just won a million dollars-just send in this form with a $100 check' come-ons amid ripped-open bills. My heart sinks. My mother is a neat-freak and methodical about paying bills on time. What is happening?

I continue to go through the house, still calling out for my mother. Finally I find her lying down in her bed, her eyes open but staring at the ceiling.

"Mom, are you all right?"

"Julie. You're here," she said, turning her head toward my voice.

"Yes, Mom. I'm here. You didn't answer the telephone so I came over. I've been looking all over the house for you. It's one o'clock. Why are you in bed? Are you sick?"

"I don't know. Help me get up: I need a hand."

"Sure, Mom." I reach out to help her swing her legs off the bed. She stands up after a minute. We begin to walk back toward the kitchen and dining room, my mother a little unsteady on her feet.

"Mom, when did you last eat?"

"I don't know."

I cringe.

"Perhaps you'd like a cup of coffee and something to eat."

"That would be nice." Then she notices the dining room table.

"What's all this?" she asks.

"That's what I was just going to ask you."

Her brow knits into a frown, and then she says,

"Oh, I remember. I think I entered the sweepstakes to get the money to pay all these bills."

I knew then that something was really wrong. My mother never fell for this kind of scam before. She has a generous pension plus

Social Security plus a hefty sum she inherited from my father. What is happening to her? What is happening to us?

Highlights:
I am worried. What does this change in behavior mean? Is it depression, infection or a form of dementia? I better call the doctor now.

STORY 2

Denial: There's Nothing Wrong with Dad

My daughter, Jane, finally calls me after I send her the email reporting my latest conversation with my husband – her father.

"There is nothing wrong with him," she shouts into the phone, "You always exaggerate!"

Here we go again, I say to myself.

"But Janie, he's confused. Yesterday, he and I took our usual walk in the neighborhood and everything seemed all right until he said, 'Where is my mother? We're at 1333 Tompkins Place.' That's the Ohio address of the house where he grew up 70 years ago, Janie!"

"Oh, Mom. You are always so critical of Dad. Something must have reminded him of his hometown roots. I bet he didn't sleep well last night."

"He slept like a log. I know 'cause you know what a light sleeper I am, waking up at all hours and making trips to the bathroom."

"Just cool it, Mom."

"Janie, he's been so forgetful lately. Why, when we came back home, he looked around as if nothing was familiar, and asked if we could eat lunch. Only it was three o'clock and we had eaten lunch only two hours before."

"Oh Mom – he's just preoccupied now that he's retired, and probably bored with nothing much to do."

"Janie, I need to remind you again: we saw the doctor. Your father is as healthy as a horse and he isn't depressed. Janie, the doctor told us that your father has early signs of dementia. That's why sometimes he is lucid but more and more often, he is not."

"Mom, you know what I think of doctors. He's wrong. Dad is just fine!"

"Janie, I know how hard it is to hear this. It's hard for me to believe it, too. But we have to face it."

Highlights:

I cannot permit someone else's denial of the truth make me doubt what I know.

STORY 3

My Brother Just Doesn't Get It!

Every time I speak to my brother, Jim, on the phone about the odd things that Mom has been saying, he accuses me of being over-critical. Yet, Mom worries me. Yesterday, Mom asked me how my kids are doing and I told her how Josh has the lead in a school play and that Andrea loves her ballet class. Then, she asked me again, and she had no recollection of what I told her before. Considering that Mom has always had a great memory, I have a gnawing feeling in my stomach.

Jim said that she probably wasn't paying attention to my answer. But, then, why did Mom ask me in the first place? Mom has always taken an interest in her grandchildren.

Last week, Mom asked me to pick up some items for her at the grocery store, and I told her I would. Then, ten minutes later, she called me and asked me to pick up the same items, seeming not to remember our earlier conversation.

It sure would help if my brother understood my concern instead of discounting my impressions. Then again, Jim never listened to my opinions, so why would he start now? But there must be something I can do to make him understand what Mom and I are going through. Even though I'm discouraged, I must keep letting him know what's going on by texting him or sending an e-mail so that we don't keep fighting on the phone. Hopefully, eventually he will see the light. Until he does, I'm going to keep talking to people who support me and respect my opinions.

Highlights:

I have to keep on reporting the facts, whether or not anyone else understands. The important thing is that *I* understand.

STORY 4

Oh, No. Not My Mother

I still can't believe it. The doctor tells me that my Mom has Alzheimer's. Panic is setting in. Sure, she has been forgetful lately, but nothing too unusual. But when she got lost going to the neighborhood supermarket where she has been shopping for years, I really got concerned. So was she. I am lucky that she agreed to have me accompany her to the doctor.

He assures us that nothing is amiss physically, no urinary tract infection to account for the changes in her behavior, or depression, which can imitate dementia. But the short-term memory problems and confusion about how to go from one place to another points to the onset of Alzheimer's.

My brother and I are in shock. My mother is, too, but not as surprised as we are. As the numbness wears off, we are left with a sense of foreboding. We are afraid that Mom will become lost to us while she is still alive. We are terrified at the thought of the journey that lies ahead.

Miraculously, Mom sits us down, her years as a therapist taking over.

"I just want you to know that we have a rocky road ahead of us. I'm not going to be the same. Soon, I am going to need you to take the lead and talk to me and to take care of me. You'll have to remind me about everything. Get someone to help out early on, so that I can get used to it. I will always want you to speak to me and treat me as if I am still alive inside because I will be."

Our eyes get wider and wider as Mom speaks. We hope she is right.

Highlights

I can't believe how sensible my mother is after hearing this diagnosis of Alzheimer's. If only I could be as wise as she is.

STORY 5

From One Extreme to Another

How can my husband be perfectly clear in one minute and then gaze off into his own world the next? Where does he go, and why does he go there? I do not understand it.

When he's coherent, I doubt the doctors, I doubt the diagnosis and I doubt myself. I say to myself: he really doesn't have Alzheimer's. Then, he struggles to speak and what he says makes no sense. Or he stares off into space, oblivious to the world around him: I want to believe that he just is daydreaming, that there's nothing really wrong.

I bring this up at my Alzheimer's caregiver support group and I see knowing nods as my eyes sweep around the circle. We begin to talk about how confused *we* feel when we see these extremes of behavior. I listen as many others tell similar stories. Relief washes over me when I hear others going through what I'm experiencing. But it's discouraging as well.

The leader explains that for someone with Alzheimer's, the connections between brain cells are clogged with debris that prevents sending one message to the next. In the beginning, some brain cells still survive to do their job, and formulate a sentence, maybe even a thought, but that other cells shut down and die. No wonder I am bewildered. How frustrating and unfair.

Highlights:
My support group helps me see that variations in intelligibility *are* part of Alzheimer's, and that my confusion is valid.

STORY 6

What About Driving?

My heart is in my mouth.

"Mom, are you sure you can drive to the supermarket?"

"Of course I can. It's Tuesday, isn't it, and I always buy groceries on Tuesdays."

She is right about that.

"I'm a careful driver, Louise," she continues.

As she says that, I see a car cut in front of her. I hold my breath, my right foot pressing sharply into the floorboard on my imaginary brake.

"Now, there's a bad driver," she says, her foot jamming on the brake in time. I exhale. She doesn't seem angry. She doesn't seem annoyed. She is relaxed, which is much more than I can say about myself.

I know we have to do a dry run with me in the car because Mom still drives, despite the onset of Alzheimer's one year ago. I read about a new evaluation system that the Division of Motor Vehicles developed and another one that neurologists use. So, I know I have to drive with her to observe how she does on these 'test' runs.

"But Mom: what about driving on Route 95?"

"I don't do that anymore, Louise. I don't feel safe on that road."

Whew. "Good decision, Mom. I get a little anxious, too, when I have to drive on the freeway."

"You should ask your brother to do the driving for you on that highway, like I do."

Highlights:
Letting someone like my Mom remain an independent driver for as long as possible can be nerve-wracking as I check up on her driving ability. I hope I can learn to enjoy the ride!

STORY 7

In Touch With Friends

As we go to a friend's house tonight, I have second thoughts. Although the other invited couple knows that my husband, John, has memory problems, they haven't seen him lately. John has trouble managing a conversation with more than one person at a time. Will he feel lost and clam up if he cannot follow what people are saying? Somehow, I always feel responsible for him, for the circumstances we're in, and for his reactions. I call Joyce, tonight's hostess and our friend for the last ten years, cluing her in that John does best with one theme at a time, one person at a time. But do the others know? Am I making a big mistake exposing him to a situation that he may have trouble handling?

We arrive and Joyce greets us.

"John. Diane. How good to see you," Joyce says, her arms outstretched. I give her a big hug, and John does, too.

"It's great to be here. How are you and Charles doing?" I ask as she guides us through the well-lit living room and out the patio door. Good. No obstacles to trip over on our way.

Charles is busy at the grill and I wonder who John can speak with one-on-one. Sara and Don, the other couple, rise up from wire-mesh chairs with a resounding,

"Diane. John. This is great! Just like the old days."

I am relieved to see that the chairs are sturdy and we sit down, our forearms resting on the arms of the chair. Joyce goes around to each of us and asks us what we would like to drink. John answers after a slight hesitation,

"Some lemonade."

Whew.

Then, Don starts to talk directly to John,

"Are you still a diehard Giants' fan?"

"Always. Is there any other team?"

And, there they are off and running about baseball, like they always do, but just a little bit slower.

I finally breathe a sigh of relief. Our wonderful friends know how to talk to John. And this night will be just fine.

Highlights:
I can keep on socializing despite this disease. My friends may be more understanding than I could ever imagine.

STORY 8

Jokes and Jokes: *That* He Remembers!

"What do women, tornadoes, and......hurricanes all have in common?"

Here it comes, again: my husband and his jokes.

I know what to expect. If I hear that joke one more time, I'll throw my coffee cup at him! Horrified by that thought, I regain control and force myself to relax.

"I don't know," I answer, knowing how much glee he will get from the punch line.

"Lots of wind," he howls, breaking into rapturous laughter.

I laugh along with him, knowing he'll be offended if I don't. Why in the world is he always telling the same jokes over and over again?

I think about our life together before Alzheimer's. He had been the life of the party, always telling lots of different jokes then, although I recall that eventually he would stop. I made it a point to never remember his tales so that I could respond as if I heard them for the first time. Now he repeats the same two jokes so often that even I memorized them.

As I ponder this, I notice that he looks at me with warmth and delight after the laughter. It occurs to me that joke-telling may be his way of saying,

'I like to laugh and make other people laugh. It's the way I reach out. Isn't this fun? And, I feel important.'

Unexpectedly I get it. This is a way he communicates! I say,

"When you tell a joke and make me laugh, I feel so close to you!"

He smiles and holds out his hand to me. I melt.

Highlights:

What a realization! Repeating jokes can be another way to maintain a loving connection. Instead of groaning inside, I am going to laugh along with him.

My Father and My Son? It's Not too Late for Me

My father has never been a communicative person. His emotional distance from me and my brother made us feel invisible when we were growing up. Often when he did speak to us, he would criticize something we did or did not do. So when my husband, I, and our ten year old son, Tommy, were invited to attend my mother's 80th birthday party gala, I was a little leery. My stomach fluttering, I dreaded what my 84 year old Dad would say, especially since he's had Alzheimer's for the last three years.

We arrive at the party held in a hotel banquet room with an outside balcony. Our place cards direct us to the table with my parents. I gear myself up for the evening.   We exchange greetings. My Dad smiles when he sees us. He never did that before. He greets Tommy with,

"Hi, son. You're big."

I raise an eyebrow. As we eat the fresh fruit appetizer, my father exclaims,

"This is good."

Another surprise. I see him glance around the table, a look of satisfaction settling in on his face. I begin to wonder – is this really my father? In my whole life, I never saw him so delighted with the family around him. All of a sudden, he gets out of his chair and says,

"So many people here. I'm going outside."

"I'll go with you, Grandpa," my son chimes in. I watch the two cross the room and step out to the balcony. I keep checking the balcony as we continue to chat with each other at the table. After about ten minutes, I decide to go outside to see how Dad and Tommy are doing. As I approach, I notice both of them looking out at the starlit sky, my Dad pointing and Tommy following his lead. I hang back, not wanting to interrupt them. I go back to the table, and wait. After about ten minutes, just as I'm about to get up again because the food has arrived, they return to the table. Tommy's eyes are shining, his lips in a broad grin.

"Grandpa's awesome, Mom," he announces. Conversation stops. "Yes. He is really awesome."

We are all speechless. A few minutes later, I ask,

"What did you two talk about?"

Glancing at my father, Tommy said,

"Grandpa told me all about the stars. He's cool." And Tommy begins to eat.

Stunned, my eyes meet my father's, and he winks at me.

Highlights:
Some changes can be unexpectedly lovely if I let go of the past.

STORY 10

There's Nothing Wrong with Me

"There's nothing wrong with me," my Mom keeps saying over and over again.

"But Mom, you just got out of the hospital an hour ago."

"Hospital? What are you talking about? I wasn't in any hospital."

That's what it's been like ever since my mother's memory began to fade. My mother has always been a fiercely independent woman. And I mean fierce. But now she has become ferocious - since she got Alzheimer's and can't remember from one minute to the next. She won't believe there's anything wrong with her.

And I worry about her all the time. She refuses medications. She barely eats. She doesn't drink enough liquids, and that probably led to the bladder infection and her hospitalization five days ago.

"Mom, I need to go to work and I can't leave you here alone."

"Don't be silly. I'm fine."

"I have Betty coming to help us. She'll be here soon."

"There's no reason for that."

"I worry about you."

"Too bad."

I am slowly approaching my limit.

"But Mom, you're having trouble walking. I want someone to stay here with you."

"I can so walk," she replies angrily, suddenly getting up and almost falling: I grab her arm to steady her.

"See what I mean, Mom?"

I am torn between her safety and her emotional well-being. I wish I had joined that Alzheimer's support group to hear how other people have faced this dilemma.

I am so frustrated. Then it occurs to me: logic doesn't work with my mother anymore.

My head tells me to overrule my mother, to find a way to get around her stubbornness. My heart aches and tells me to back off, wait a few minutes, and try once more.

Do I wait for a crisis to over-rule her wishes? Suddenly, I think to myself: this hospital stay was a crisis. Her almost falling is a crisis. I have to follow my instincts and insist right now. Again. Gently. Despite her objections.

Highlights:

I am the one who can think straight. I must make sound decisions, even if it means overruling my mother.

STORY 11

So Now She's Nice to Me!

My mother. Some days that phrase fills me with despair. What a burden she is. All my life she yelled at me and disapproved of the choices I made when I was growing up. Now she has become agreeable as Alzheimer's descends on her. Well, my memory is very much intact. And I remember those thoughtless and mean things she sometimes said to me. Yet I, her daughter, am the one she turns to now. What nerve. I want to continue to dislike her, but how can I feel that way toward this pleasant sick old woman who needs to be cared for?

As I approach her, a hot cup of coffee in one hand and a plate of buttered cinnamon toast in the other, she sniffs the aromas, looks up from staring mindlessly out in space, sees the food and bursts into a welcome smile.

"Is that for me?" she asks, shyly.

"Of course, Mom."

"You are so kind. I am so lucky to have you. Thank you."

How can I object to this woman when she is now so gracious and nice to me? I sigh. How ironic that Alzheimer's has made her into the mother I always longed for.

Highlights:
Alzheimer's has changed my mother into the mother I always wanted.

Repetitions are Exhausting

I am worn out. If I hear him repeat himself one more time, I'll scream. It is so aggravating. Why does he do that? I keep telling him that he doesn't have to go to work today, that he retired as an insurance agent years ago, and he keeps on saying,

"I have to go out. I must go to work today," his voice insistent.

Can't he understand what I say just once?

Then he starts to rummage through his dresser, and clothes that I had neatly folded now are strewn along the dull blue carpet. I want to grab him, shake him, and make him stop.

Now, both of us are upset. Great. What should I do? What should I say?

I stop for a moment. One of us has to think clearly.

I ask myself: why is he searching through the dresser, repeating the same words over and over again? What do his actions mean?

He's looking through his clothes to get ready. When he worked, he felt important. For over 30 years, work was his anchor, the source of his self-esteem. He was successful then, and proud of himself.

Is that it? Does he need to feel important and worthwhile? If so, going through the motions the way he used to is his way to feel that he has a purpose. I suddenly no longer feel so frustrated. I change my approach.

"Honey, I think you miss working. You were so good at it."

He stops rummaging and looks up at me.

"No wonder you want to go to work today."

He looks surprised, and we start to talk. For a little while.

Highlights:
It is exhausting when I have to figure out the meaning of his repeated words and behavior. But when I stop and try to understand, we connect.

STORY 13

I Feel Lonely

I feel lonely. Even though I am always with my husband, I feel lonely. I miss the way we used to talk. I miss the way we used to be.

Our special time used to be the morning, both of us sitting down for a cup of coffee, each taking a different newspaper and we would read the highlights to each other.

"Make sure to catch Thomas Friedman in today's *Times*."

"I'll just wait 'til next week and read it in the local paper."

And then, he'd look up and smile: we loved to tease each other about which paper was superior.

But this morning unfolds as I knew it would. He can hardly read the newspaper now, and after a few minutes, he puts it down. I persist in reading the *Times* but I'm distracted: the kitchen echoes with silence interspersed with slurps of coffee. I keep remembering the past, not wanting to face the present. But face it I must.

Highlights:
I feel such an ache whenever I recall the 'good old days'. It's hard to accept him as he is today.

STORY 14

Gazing Out the Window

Today when I look at my wife, I notice that she is gazing into seeming nothingness outside the window.

"What are you looking at, dear?" I ask. She doesn't answer.

Where is she, I wonder, feeling bewildered from not knowing, feeling the ache of remembering the past. I want to be close to her. I pull over a straight-backed chair, sit down beside her, and find myself looking outside with her. The bottle brush tree, ablaze with red blossoms, gently waves its branches, almost as a greeting. A hummingbird lands on thin air up close to the bristles of the flower, hovering, suspended, its wings flapping so fast, almost invisibly. How does that bird manage to suspend itself on a bed of air without tumbling to the ground?

I wish I could be as sure of myself as that hummingbird. I beat my wings without feeling any balance, not knowing what supports me as I muddle through caring for my wife. Not knowing what she is experiencing.

Slowly I reach out for her hand. I feel her delicate, cool, and spindly fingers settle in around mine. And I know that we are sharing something special in this moment, gazing out the window. Together. Love washes over me.

Highlights:
Like the hummingbird, I will have faith that our love remains steady amid the ups and downs of this disease.

STORY 15

La Traviata: The Lost Woman

Lost. La Traviata. Puccini. That is me today, too.

I have an urge to listen to *La Traviata,* not only because the glorious music elevates me into a joyous state, but because the translation of the title is "The Lost Woman," such an apt description of my wife. Only, I think that Puccini was thinking of love, not dementia, when he wrote that opera.

I walk over to the CD player, a disc in hand, insert it, and push the play button. The music begins: the overture a recap of joy and sorrow. Puccini brings haunting beauty to the state of loss.

Yes, I am lost, as well. My wife is losing her memory, and I am losing her. I am losing the woman I fell in love with 45 years ago, as she is losing herself.

The rich baritone of Robert Merrill fills the air. The soprano voice of Roberta Peters celebrates the life of the courtesan. They were married once in real life, I muse. Suddenly I hear another voice singing along with music. I look up to see my wife rising from the chair, the empty look in her eyes vanishing. She looks like her former animated self. Her hands start to sway back and forth as she sings and hums along with Roberta Peters. On cue, I begin to join Robert Merrill, the four of us engrossed as we soar to new heights.

Maybe we are not so lost after all.

Highlights:
Music can bypass the conscious brain and contact the heart to help me and my soul mate connect. I cherish these moments.

Like It Or Not

I arrive at the caregiver support meeting and need to speak about what I have been mulling over.

"You know, in the beginning when I first heard about my husband's diagnosis, I was in shock. Numb. I kept thinking, not him, not us. But now I find myself making peace with how this has affected us."

"But hasn't he changed for the worse? I know my father has."

"Of course he has changed. We used to say to each other, 'There is nothing so constant as change.' It's true - we weren't thinking of Alzheimer's when we agreed about that."

"So now what do you think about how he has changed?"

"As my heart remembers the way he used to be, and I do suffer as he suffers, I now can reflect back and realize that in the past, we survived other changes. Didn't we always have to face the times he would get a job or lose one, move from our first cramped apartment into a spacious house, adjust to the two of us become parents of three children? Each one of these events made us reassess how we looked at ourselves, how we acted, how we dealt with and adapted to our new responsibilities."

"How can you compare that to what's going on now?"

"Just as we succeeded in adjusting to these changes in the past, we're doing that now. We still are linked together, but in an unusual way. The love that bound us from the beginning is still there between us. But it's different. And for the first time ever, now I treasure every moment that we share."

Highlights:

I am learning to make peace with the changes that keep on happening to us, and treasure the moments we have together.

PART II

On The Home Front: Stirring the Oatmeal

We've known each other a long time,
You and me.
With ups and downs,
Laughter and pain,
Hanging in throughout
And now it is time
To keep on
Stirring the oatmeal, my love.
For if I do not,
It will surely burn.
So stir I must,
Even though my hand aches
I must keep on
Stirring the oatmeal.

Judith London 2012

Where Are Your Going? The Great Escape

The red, yellow, and blue spines of the books are carefully arranged on the bookshelves in the colorful poster and they make an impressive decorating statement on the front door. I just hope they will stop my mother from opening it. I had read that disguising a door with a poster deters those with Alzheimer's from wandering out of the house.

The last time my mother slipped out, prior to the door remodel, my ears picked up the click-clack of the latch as it automatically closed. I dropped a dish towel, rushed to the front of the house, and grabbed my keys as I opened the door. I followed her to see if she knew where she was going.

Mom walked determinedly. Confident at first, gradually she began to glance around and even stumble on the sidewalk, puzzled, unsure. Then I saw that she was about to step off the curb, ignoring the red stop signal. I reached her just in time.

"Mom, you stepped off the curb when the light was red."

"Oh. "

"Where are you going, Mom?"

"I want to get some coffee."

"But Mom, I told you I was making coffee in the kitchen."

"Oh."

"Let's go back, Mom. The coffee will be ready by the time we return."

"But I want to take a walk," she said, forgetting about the coffee.

"That's a great idea, Mom. I'll join you," I said, linking my right arm with hers.

After ten minutes of circling around the block, we were back at the house. As I opened the door, my mother stepped in and said,

"Oh, good. I smell coffee."

That's when I bought the poster and a dead bolt for the front door.

Highlights:
By taking some simple precautions to protect someone who wanders, I can breathe a sigh of relief.

STORY 18

Golf Anyone? Once You Get Him Started…

Today is a beautiful day – not too hot and the air smells sweet: a perfect day for golf. I remember the old days when my husband, Charlie, and I would look at each other on a day like today and at the same moment exclaim, "Golf!"

Charlie was so good at it; he just loved that sport. But that was B.A. – Before Alzheimer's. I ache when I think about all we keep losing now.

I think to myself, why can't we enjoy the day anyhow? I take a chance and proclaim,

"Charlie, we are going to the driving range today."

A bewildered look spreads across his face. My heart sinks as I realize that he does not remember what a driving range is. Golf had been his passion. But now?

"It's all right," I hastily reply. I want to play golf. I need you to keep me company, and it's a perfect day for me to swing a few."

His face relaxes. Miraculously, he allows me to help him get ready without a struggle. What a relief.

We get into the car and head for the driving range.

When we arrive, I make the arrangements. Finally, I set the ball down on the rubber tee, the sweet scent of freshly mowed grass tickling my nostrils. I keep hoping that this is a good idea. I place his fingers around the handle of the driver.

Without hesitation, his veined fingers finish closing around the club, and he swings away the way he always did, the ball sailing out 200 yards. I am astonished. So is he.

He turns to me and smiles with exultation, the deep frown of a few minutes before melting away.

After three more drives, he begins to slow down.

I sit him down on a nearby bench.

"My turn now," I say.

After a few swings, I join him on the bench. I feel exhilarated. He reaches out for my hand. My heart skips a beat like in the old days. After a while, I say,

"Let's do it again."

Slowly Charlie gets up, follows me, takes the club I place in his hand, and assumes his stance. He swings at that ball with renewed vigor, and it disappears into the great beyond. My heart soars.

Highlights:
Once you get him started, he may still know how to do something he could do years before. What a thrill.

STORY 19

Where are My Keys?

As usual, I'm in a hurry. I'm late for an appointment and still scurrying around. My father, with memory problems, is ready. I'm not.

So here I stand, all set to go out the door with him when I look in my hand and shudder: no house keys. No car keys. My father sits patiently on the bench by the front door watching me. I mutter, not too loud because I don't want him to hear the names I'm calling myself.

I rush back to the bedroom: no luck on the dresser. I dart into the hall and run to the kitchen. No sign of them there. I retrace my steps and jerk open the door of the hall closet, praying they're in the pocket of my sweatshirt. Nope.

All this time, my father good-naturedly observes me, quizzically, one eye brow slightly raised, the way he used to when I was a kid and frantic. Finally, I turn to him, in exasperation.

"Dad, I just can't find my keys. I forgot where I put them, and now we are going to be late!"

His eyes twinkling, my father replies, "You mean I'm not the only one who forgets things!" He begins to chuckle.

I stop in my tracks and can't help but smile. He laughs louder, and suddenly, I laugh along with him, the two of us bent over, tears in our eyes.

After we both calm down, he quietly says, "Check your purse."

"I did already, but OK, I'll look again."

I thrust my hand into the bottomless pit of the sac that I call a purse, which is as large a horse's feed bag, when behold! My fingers curl around my set of keys. I look up sheepishly and say, "Dad, what would I do without you?"

Highlights:
Sometimes I just have to laugh and know that I forget, too.

STORY 20

The Midnight Wanderer

I am exhausted. How can I get more sleep, I ask myself.

My wife tires, too. After her busy day of activities at the Adult Day Care Center today, she falls asleep early – before eight o'clock. I sigh and say to myself: I better be on watch tonight because she definitely will wake up in the middle of the night and commence her wandering routine. She'll go from room to room like a detective on the prowl, and then jiggle the knob on the front door, fortunately, to no avail.

I had to learn her routine the hard way. One night I awoke to find her no longer beside me. The front door that I knew I had locked was ajar. I was some sight racing down the driveway in pajamas, not feeling the rough concrete surface scratching my bare feet, my heart pounding with fear in the middle of the night. I spotted her strolling down the block, caught up with her, and steered her back into the house.

After that incident, I installed the double-keyed dead bolt lock on all the doors that lead to the outside and I keep the key around my neck at all times. At least I don't have to worry about her leaving the house any more. I pray that I will find her somewhere inside the house in time if something terrible like a fire breaks out.

Maybe I will go to sleep early, too. I set my watch alarm clock for one a.m.

I settle myself in bed, my wife snoring right beside me. I finally fall asleep but on some level I know that when I stop hearing that nasal 'shnuckling' sound she makes, I'd better wake up, alarm or no alarm. I try to sleep, but it's hard because I am still troubled about what she might do. I can't close off every room of the house because of her need to roam.

Finally, my eyes close. I dream that I sit contentedly in meditation in a monastery. I revel in the quiet. It is <u>too</u> quiet. I get up with a start and look at the illuminated dial of my watch: 12:30 a.m. My wife is gone. Off by a half-hour.

I throw back the covers, jam my feet into well-worn slippers, and grab my robe. I begin the trek around the house from one room to another, calling out her name. Then I notice a light coming from the kitchen. My wife is standing in the middle of the room, brows knitted together and looking around as if this was the first time she'd ever seen a kitchen.

"Joanie, what are you doing?" I say, as I sense myself shifting from relief to exasperation.

"I'm hungry."

It would be futile to tell her it's too early for breakfast so let's go back to bed. A sudden inspiration floods through my mind. I say,

"Joanie, I have an idea. Let's have some milk and cookies." Her face lights up, her eyes crinkle and she grins.

"Sit down and join me," I continue, and I smile back, my irritation disappearing.

We both relish every mouthful of butter cookies (I was afraid that if I gave her anything with chocolate in it, the caffeine would keep her up the rest of the night) and sip warm milk. When we are finished, she looks up at me, belches, yawns and says,

"I'm sleepy."

"Me too."

I get up from the table, put the glasses into the sink, and say, "Let's go to bed."

She stands up and I walk over to her, my arms outstretched. Joanie nestles in for a big hug, murmuring, "Ummm." It feels good. We stroll together, arms linked, retracing our steps back to the bedroom, and I tuck her in. I think to myself, who would believe that milk and cookies, that old stand-by, would get her back into bed?

As I lay down beside her, I hear that familiar, soft 'shnuckling' sound and it gradually becomes louder. I smile to myself. In all the years we've been together, I never would have thought that my wife snoring would give me such pleasure.

Highlights:

I am amazed that cookies and milk work wonders for my midnight wanderer. And, to think that snoring would reassure me that all is well.

STORY 21

The Next Ride in the Car

Back in the car again. I am always uneasy every time I have to take this ride. It's been two years since Mom was diagnosed with Alzheimer's. But taking trial runs with my mother as the driver follows the Division of Motor Vehicle guidelines on how to determine if a person is a safe driver, so I have to do it.

"Where are we going again, Mom?"

"The grocery store."

"What do you need to buy, Mom?"

"I don't exactly know. I'll figure it out."

This is not like my mother. She has always made a list of what she needs, and follows it accurately.

"Do you have a list with you, Mom?"

"What list?"

"The shopping list."

"Oh."

As she says that, she suddenly switches to the right lane without looking in the rear view mirror. I sit upright, alarmed. She seems oblivious to what she just did. This is one of the warning signs I read about. Could this be the last time she drives? Luckily, the supermarket is at the intersection.

"Turn right, Mom, and we'll be there."

"I know that!" she replies, making a wide right turn. A parking space opens up, and she manages to park the car. Over the line.

After shopping, an adventure in itself as my Mom struggles to remember what she needs to buy, I say,

"You know, Mom, let's make a stop at that new bakery that opened. You've never been there before but I think you'll like it. They even serve coffee and have delicious muffins. I'll drive since I know the way."

"Oh, you know how much I love muffins. Okay, here are the car keys."

I breathe easier. Mission accomplished.

Highlights:

I know Mom may become angry or insulted, but I need to make sure she no longer drives now that I see she has lost the ability to be aware of her limitations.

STORY 22

Monday is Wash Day

The two of us sit down together at the faded blue speckled Formica kitchen table. I don't know much about folding the laundry, but my wife still does. I decide to learn how to do it now before it is too late.

"Dear, can you help me with the laundry? I just took the clothes from the dryer and I don't know how to fold them properly."

I place a once-white tee shirt in her hand. She lays it down on the table and comments,

"Soft, isn't it?" Then she inhales.

"Smells so fresh."

"That's because I used the fabric softener you told me about."

"I did? Well, that was a good idea."

I watch as she smoothes out the garment several times, her eyebrows drawn together in deep thought. I take another tee shirt from the laundry basket, place it on the table, and follow her lead. Then, she makes a fold along the side of the shirt, and runs her fingers over the crease. I do the same. Moving to the other side, she continues,

"You fold it here, too," her voice assumes the air of authority she had when she taught nursing students years ago.

"Now, fold the bottom back."

She deftly flips the shirt back onto the table, looks up at me and smiles, satisfied with the end result. And so am I.

Highlights:
When I focus on things she still can do, we both feel better. And I can learn what I, eventually, will have to do.

STORY 23

The Walk Around the Lake

An onlooker would smile and say to herself, how sweet they are. Growing old together and sharing a walk around the glistening lake. She would have no clue how hard it was to arrive at this moment.

My husband has Alzheimer's, you see. I began the tedious preparation hours before, getting him up and dressed, fed, cajoling him to cooperate so that I could bring him to this place we've always loved. And we've made it.

We savor the moment, strolling along like young lovers, holding hands, our feet crunching on the tree-lined gravel path that encircles the shimmering lake. The filtered sunlight lights up parts of our faces, and his features look like pieces of a jigsaw puzzle.

"See the blue flowers on the rosemary," I say, gently squeezing his hand as I point to a shrub.

His graying eyes follow my cue and see where I point. He smiles.

"Let's pick a sprig and smell it." With that, I reach out, snap off a twig and hold it to my nose, then to his, the sharp fragrance tickling our nostrils as we inhale.

"I love your rosemary chicken," he says as his memory awakens.

He speaks an entire sentence, something he has not done for months. How I have missed that. My face registers surprise, then delight. Eyes misting over, I tell him,

"I love the sound of your voice. And we'll have rosemary chicken for dinner tonight."

Highlights:
When something I do awakens his memory, it is a victory over Alzheimer's.

STORY 24

The Dinner Table

As I watch my wife standing in the kitchen, getting ready to set the table, she holds the fork in her right hand, glances tentatively at the table top, and places the fork to the right of the dinner plate. Her face grimaces and a look of consternation spreads across it. She picks up the same fork, grasps it in her hand, and after silently moving her lips, tentatively puts it down, this time to the left side of the plate. Her frown deepens. She picks it up a third time, surveys the table, and reluctantly places the fork on its side directly on the plate, her brow still furrowed, sensing that something is wrong, but finally letting go of the silverware. She raises her clear brown eyes to meet mine, her eyebrows now arched, looking for my approval. She gives me a half-hearted grin, knowing that she didn't get it right.

"Honey, let me show you what you taught me years ago."

I set down the silverware next to another plate the way she always used to do it: the fork to the left side, the knife and spoon to the right side. I continue,

"Let's do the next one together."

I place my hand gently over hers, and together we pick up the fork, and put it down. "See, it matches the other setting." Using the same method, we pick up the other pieces of silverware, one at a time, and place them properly, my hand over hers. She is aware of my touch and I feel the softness of her skin. We look up at each other and smile.

Highlights:
I miss my wife, who, for so long, had been my equal partner. But I tell myself to acknowledge her as she is today, and savor the moment.

STORY 25

What Happened to
The Laundry?

Today I decide to encourage my wife to be helpful and use up some of her restless energy. I dump out a small load of clean clothes onto the kitchen table, and say,

"Honey, how about folding these while I go outside and mow the lawn?"

"Okay."

"See you in a half hour," I add, pointing to my watch.

When I return, there is no sign of the laundry.

"Honey, where are the clothes you folded?" She looks at me puzzled and says,

"What clothes?"

I'm beginning to feel sorry that I asked her to do this chore in the first place.

"I gave them to you before I went out back. Where did you put them?" I am getting annoyed.

"I don't know."

I hurry off to the bedroom, but there is no sign of the items. I check the dresser drawers. Nothing. I think about where else she could have put them. She was still in the kitchen when I came back inside so I return there and look around again. Everything appears to be in order. I decide to get a cold drink having worked up a sweat. When I open the cabinet for a glass, I see two sets of perfectly paired socks in between the glassware. Then I open the refrigerator and there is my underwear neatly folded on a rack.

"Honey, look at what I just found!" And as I show her where the missing laundry ended up, we both begin to laugh.

Highlights:
When I can see the humor in a trying situation, it relieves the tension.

STORY 26

Visiting Grandpa

We drive up to the Tudor house, the peeling white exterior crying out to be painted. My mother greets us after she opens the heavy, scuffed, dark oak door. I notice the sun bleached drapes stirring but the fresh air wafting in from the open dining room window doesn't quite disguise the musty odor of the 50 year old house. My parents, Dad, 84 and battling Alzheimer's, and Mom, 78, sometimes battling with Dad, both refuse to budge from their longtime home.

Once, the house echoed with the sounds of me and my brothers playing on the diamond design of the Tabriz rug. The Chippendale chairs in the dining room created a wonderful obstacle course which had been a major source of amusement for us as children on rainy days.

But now my sons, 10 and 12, full of energy until the moment their grandmother appears at the front door, become silent. As we enter, the boys eye the playing possibilities longingly through the open doorway to that pale green dining room, but restrain themselves as they catch my eye and I slowly shake my head 'no'.

"Grandpa is in the living room," my mother says as she leads us in.

As the boys settle onto the deep pillows of the worn velvet sofa, they wonder – why do we have to come here? Grandpa doesn't even recognize us. My father sits on a sturdy black leather arm chair that looks a little out of place among the deeply-upholstered club chairs, the thick pillows sagging from the many years seating guests in comfort.

The boys fidget and glance up at the shelves on the opposite wall, shelves filled with so many books that they think they are in a public library. Fragments of gold letters along some of the bindings glint in the light. The boys want to get a closer look, but aren't sure they should.

"It's all right, guys. You can go take a look and pull out a book if you'd like."

Now that my mother gives them permission, they jump up off the sofa, scamper across the flowers of the faded Oriental rug and head for the books. They gaze at the frayed bindings, until one of the books catches the eye of the older boy. He slides out the faded blue volume, hesitates, and then walks tentatively over to his grandfather.

"Grandpa, this book has your name written on it. The title is *The Paths to Greatness*. Did you write this?" asks the boy, his tone incredulous.

My father snaps out of his reverie, looks at the book, and back to the boys, seeing them for the first time since they arrived, and replies, "Why, yes. I think I did."

Then, grandfather and his grandsons, their heads forming a triangle, look down in unison as the elder boy begins to turn the yellowed pages and reads aloud the faded print.

I beam for all three of them.

Highlights:
My kids may be young, but they do have the ability to connect with my Dad. When they visit their grandfather, unexpected moments of delight may unfold.

STORY 27

The Shop-At-Home Service

"Hi Mom. Today we are going shopping."

My mother perks up at this announcement. She loves to shop. Only now, I can't bring her into a store without losing her. She darts from counter to counter, me running after her, the whole scene just too stimulating for her and too harrowing for me. So I have decided to create the Betty Boutique Shop-At-Home Service.

I solicited donations from my friends, items in decent condition that are only slightly used. I saved up some cardboard boxes to serve as the "sale" repository. I sorted out the items I'd accumulated, scarves in one bin, purses in another, sweaters and blouses in the next. I even collected some stuffed animals and fleece throws. I pre-arranged everything on a long table in the living room.

"Betty's Boutique is open for business!"

Mom and I enter the room and her face lights up. She begins to rummage through the contents of one carton, chooses a few items, and then moves on to the next one. I do the same, and ask her,

"Do you think this is a good color for me?"

"The blue one is better. You always look good in blue."

"You do have an eye for these things, Mom."

When we come to the stuffed animals, we both laugh. I pick up a soft Teddy bear and begin to stroke it. Mom says,

"Can I have that one?"

I give it to her and she says,

"It's so soft. Like your skin when you were a baby."

I smile and say,

"It reminds me of the softness of your cheek, Mom."

And it does.

Highlights:
When I re-create a situation at home that Mom used to love and she responds, I feel close to her.

STORY 28

Why Are You Taking Off Your Clothes?

Here it is - another day where I have to go through the morning ritual: getting my father dressed. He begins to remove his shirt right after I've just put it on.

"Dad, stop taking off your clothes."

He sits on the edge of the bed, and keeps on tugging away at the top three buttons of the shirt. This is annoying. My voice goes up one decibel.

"Dad, why are you doing that? You just chose that shirt!"

He doesn't even blink at me, nor say one word. His hands grope around the collar to pull the shirt off, his face contorted. I feel the anger rising and my cheeks becoming blotchy. I take three deep breaths. Somehow, I realize that I have to stop raising my voice.

I think for a minute and ask myself, why would he want to take off his shirt? Maybe it irritates his skin. Maybe he is too hot. Maybe he is restless and doesn't know what to do with his fingers. I inhale deeply again, slowly exhale, and decide on a different approach. Gently, I place my hand on his back and say,

"Dad, are you itchy? Is that why you want to remove this shirt?" He looks up at me, and shakes his head, no.

"Are you too warm? Here is another one."

He pushes my hand with the new shirt away.

"Is this shirt too tight?" He stops for a few seconds, then resumes tugging at the collar.

"I think that shirt is uncomfortable around your neck, Dad. Let me help you unbutton the top few buttons."

He nods and says, "Okay."

Highlights:

It may take me a while, but I finally remember to stop, look and listen to my Dad. Then I realize: his actions speak louder than the words he cannot say.

STORY 29

The Magic of Shakespeare

We sit down quietly, nestled in our living room that wraps around us like a cozy blanket. My wife stares off in space, not really conscious of where we are. Nostalgic for the many hours we eagerly anticipated spending an evening this way, I rise, and walk over to our shelves jammed with books. I don't know which one to pull out. One catches my eye and the volume of Shakespearean sonnets finally gives way to my tugging. I open to a memorable passage. I gently call my wife's name and begin to read aloud,

"Shall I compare thee to a summer's day?
Thou art more lovely and more temperate."

I stop and recall how thrilled she used to be when I read those words to her. She had been a high school English teacher, then, and delighted in making Shakespeare come alive for her students. I look up from reading, softly calling out her name again. Would she, could she, remember and understand that this sonnet is my way of saying how much I love her despite this disease?

I continue,
> "Rough winds do shake the darling buds of May,
> Sometime too hot the eye of heaven shines,
> And often is his gold complexion dimmed;
> And every fair from fair sometimes declines,
> By chance or nature's changing course untrimmed."

Slowly, she turns her gaze away from seeing nothingness and her eyes begin to search for mine.
> "But thy eternal summer shall not fade
> Nor lose possession of that fair thou ow'st;
> Nor shall death brag thou wand'rest in his shade,

Her face gradually transforms as I continue to read: her blank stare fades and her eyes light up. My voice begins to tremble as I reach the last part.
> "When in eternal lines to time thou grow'st,
> So long as men can breathe, or eyes can see,
> So long lives this, and this gives life to thee."

She rises from her chair, tears glistening in her eyes, and comes over to me, her arms outstretched. I stand up to be swept up in her embrace, my body melting into warmth and love.

Highlights:
With a reminder from the past, we can still share magical moments amid all the pain and longing.

PART III

Stress: Release Valves

I need to anticipate
The stress that gets to me.
As it creeps up,
Invisible at first
'Til one day
I am
Overwhelmed.
Too far along
To figure out
what to do.

I need to anticipate
How to cope
Before I am
Overcome.

Judith London 2012

STORY 30

I Give You Thursdays

The face of the tall stately man is relaxed and smiling. He is wearing crisp khaki slacks and a pressed light blue shirt. Confidently, he strides over to the Alzheimer's Association table at the Senior Expo.

"I have Alzheimer's," he announces cheerfully to me as I sit behind the desk.

Surprised, I say,

"Well we have wonderful information that can help, sir."

"There's my wife, Shirley," he said, pointing to a tall, slender woman with a harried look on her face. "She's the one you should talk to."

He picks up some hand-outs, places them in a royal blue tote bag with the words "Main Street Bank" emblazoned in white letters and continues on to the next table.

A few moments later, Shirley stops by. I say,

"I believe I just met your husband. He is so friendly."

"I know. He's had Alzheimer's for two years and can hold a conversation for a half hour. My friends don't really believe that he has it."

Nevertheless, Shirley has the tell-tale signs of an exhausted caregiver. With a drawn face, she nervously glances around to locate her husband's whereabouts.

She continues in a strained voice, "At home he follows me wherever we go, but I know that if we are in an enclosed space with other people, he can go off by himself."

"How are you managing?"

Tears come into her eyes.

"We've been married for 48 years. Now, my life has changed. I am devastated."

"It must be so hard for you."

"My children tell me, 'Mom. You are so sad.' I ask you, how am I supposed to be? Thank Goodness I started to attend those Alzheimer's Association support groups for caregivers or I would be completely lost."

"That's good. And you could use some time for yourself to replenish your energy."

"I wouldn't know what to do with myself alone. We've been together for so long."

"It must be scary to do things by yourself when you're not used to it. Could you call a friend or someone in that support group, and go out for a cup of coffee or a walk?"

"It's not so easy to make those phone calls."

"I know. Maybe it will get easier to reach out once you make the first move."

"My husband and I can still go to those free concerts all summer long. And, I am taking an art class by myself. I can still leave him for a little while if I sit him down in front of the T.V. – that always works," Shirley adds, hopefully.

I don't want to tell her that T.V. works only for so long. Instead I say,

"Good. You know, now would be a good time to have someone help you out."

"Oh, my sons come to visit us."

"Yes, but perhaps you could ask them to stay, instead of cooking and entertaining them."

A knowing look crosses her face.

I continue, "I read somewhere that on his mother's birthday, her son wrote on the birthday card, 'I give you the gift of Thursday every week for me to stay with Dad so you can have a much-needed break. I love you both.' Shirley: why don't you pretend it's your birthday, and ask for this present now?"

Highlights:
I won't wait until it's my birthday. I will ask for my present early: someone to relieve me.

STORY 31

Why Won't You Listen to Me?

"Tom, put on your shirt."

No response from my husband.

"Tom, here is the shirt. Please put it on," I repeat myself, my voice a notch higher. My husband has a perplexed look on his face.

"Thomas, here is the shirt. PUT IT ON NOW!"

He looks up at me, his eye brows scrunched together, knitted into a deep frown; the edges of his mouth droop down. Finally he says,

"Stop yelling at me."

"But I keep TELLING you to PUT ON THE SHIRT and you won't budge."

The hurt look deepens on his face, and I start to feel ashamed of myself but I can't control how angry I feel. Why is it so hard for me to believe that he can't help himself? Why do I berate him?

That's when I realize that it's really about me, too. I can't accept that this former prince of a man cannot follow a simple direction. I think: I cannot deal with one more frustrating day. Then, I begin to feel contrite. I pick up the shirt and say,

"Forgive me for yelling at you, Tom. Now, let's slip your arm through the sleeve." I take his arm, and he extends it to me. He slides his arm through, turns his body and automatically searches for the second sleeve, and finds it on his own. He turns back facing me, and I say,

"Now, let's button it. I'll do the first one."

Once I begin, he continues to button the rest of the shirt completely on his own.

Highlights:

I need to forgive myself for being so impatient and angry. I realize that once I lead the way and initiate what needs to be done, my husband follows what I do. For now.

STORY 32

Bills, Bills, Bills

I burst into tears. I cannot bear opening up one more medical bill. Why did my father have to get Alzheimer's? Why am I the only one stuck with taking care of all of this? My brother does nothing. Oh, in a nice way, he apologizes and says he's too far away, but I've had it.

I reach for the phone and dial, swallowing my tears.

"Josh? I need help."

I start to tear up again.

"Diane, what's wrong? Is it Dad?"

I struggle to find my voice.

"It's me and it's Dad. Josh, I just can't manage all the paperwork on top of taking care of him. I'm at the end of my rope."

Silence.

"Josh, I need help. I know that I always want to be in charge of everything with Dad but it's just too much. Please. There must be something you can do."

"Well, I…"

"Financial stuff comes so easy for you. We both share the power of attorney. Josh, can you handle some of this? I am so sorry that I've kept this to myself for so long."

The clock keeps ticking away as he mulls that over. Finally, he says,

"I suppose I could pay the bills. What's involved?"

He can hear me sigh, or is it a gasp?

"Well, there's the doctor statements, then the home health aides…" and I start to rattle off the drugs my Dad takes as I stare at the pile of papers on my kitchen table. I stop and take a deep breath.

"Diane. Why don't you put all those bills into an overnight mailing envelope and send them to me? When I receive them, I'll call you if I can't figure it out myself."

Relief washes over me. I didn't think it would be so simple.

"Josh, I feel so much better now. You are a great brother. Truly."

Highlights:
When I overcome my resistance to asking for help, I find people more willing to help out than I thought.

STORY 33

Stop Yelling at Me

Today is a day where there is nothing I can do or say that will make my father stop yelling every five minutes. I thought his mood would shift when he ate his favorite breakfast, Swiss cheese and eggs, but he resumed his nastiness after the last sip of coffee. You know – saying things like, "Leave me alone. You're mean. Go away."

Yet, I have been kind and accommodating all along. I sigh. I feel terrible. I feel unappreciated. This is one day that the routine of brushing his teeth and getting him dressed just isn't worth the hassle. So what if he looks rumpled today.

I think about what would make me feel better, instead of what would make him feel better. I close my eyes and take a few deep breaths. Don't take it personally, I say over and over to myself. I see that I need a break today and I call up my uncle.

"Uncle Lou. He's having a bad day today and so am I."

"So sorry to hear that."

"I know today is your day off but I am desperate. If you could only come over even for an hour or two. I've got to get out of this house!"

"You know, I could rearrange some things and come over around two o'clock. Would that help?"

"It would make all the difference to me."

I am so glad that I heard myself so that I could ask for help.

Highlights:
Whether Dad is upset or OK, I realize that I must reach out for help and make time just for me.

STORY 34

Compassion

Compassion means sympathy for the suffering of others, often accompanied by a desire to help. That's me. There's no question that I am filled with compassion for my father with Alzheimer's.

My compassion permeates my attitude and takes form as deeds: laying out his clothes the night before, greeting him with a smile, helping him dress in the morning. I make sure he washes up, brushes his teeth, and combs his hair. I prepare his meals. You get the picture.

After I make breakfast, we sit together to eat as if nothing is out of the ordinary. But conversation is a challenge. He no longer talks spontaneously. The burden of discussion falls completely on me. I rack my brain for something to say, finally choosing the obvious: food.

This stimulates him to say something. I agree with whatever he says; why argue? He sees the world through his lens, not mine. I'm glad he speaks and I struggle to figure out what he is trying to convey when still recognizable words string along but make no sense.

Sometimes I bring up something about the past, something that meant something to him at one time. And so it goes on throughout the day, day after day, week after week, month after month. And then he gets worse.

Eventually, my compassion wears down. When he begins to resist my help, compassion evaporates. Patience disappears. My energy wanes. I am drained. Annoyed.

I get angry with him. Then, I get angry with myself.

I just cannot feel for my father 24/7. It's too much for me: it has nothing to do with my love for him. I realize think that no caregiver can sustain that depth of compassion when caring continually for anyone with Alzheimer's disease or any dementia.

Then it hits me: maybe I need some compassion for myself. What a mind-boggling thought.

I think about this for a while and consider: how can I show some compassion for myself, for the burden I face? Maybe I should accept my feelings, even the unpleasant ones. Maybe I need to do something just for me.

Highlights:
We are all simply human, with human limitations. I can have compassion for my father *and* I can have compassion for myself as well.

STORY 35

I'm Not Doing So Well

Today, as the day wears on, it is me who is feeling out of sorts. In contrast, my wife is in surprisingly good spirits. This morning, she lets me help her get washed and dressed, and even set the table. I only give her spoons, since instant oatmeal with brown sugar is on the menu. (I have noticed that she isn't chewing her food carefully before she swallows, and don't want her to choke on dry cereal.) She places one spoon where she usually sits and one on the opposite side for me.

After we eat breakfast, she begins to trail me around the house. It irritates me.

"Stop following me: I have to go to the bathroom."

Then she marches right in to the bathroom after I enter it. I stop and guide her back out.

"Here. I have something for you to read."

I place a "Good Housekeeping" magazine in her lap and tell her to stay put.

I never thought that a simple "pee" would become a luxury.

I am so tired of taking care of her, but I can't tell that to anyone. People would think I'm selfish. Uncaring. But it's so hard, day after day, with no relief and no improvement of her condition in sight.

I still miss going to work. At least, there I was doing something that I enjoyed. I know that I should be grateful that I have a pension, but somehow, retirement is not supposed to be this way. I miss the way life used to be.

I've been resisting those Alzheimer's support groups for caregivers. Probably a bunch of women. But this is getting to me and I need to talk.

Highlights:
Like it or not, I need to share what I'm going through. Despite my discomfort about speaking up.

STORY 36

Tears and Touch

Another day and I wonder – how will my mother be? Will she be happy or sad? Will she be cooperative or upset? One thing I know for sure: she'll be confused. Will I be able to find that spark within her? Because my experience tells me that when I do, we connect, and I feel so much better.

But things are tough for her today. I'm in for a rough day.

"Mom, why are you crying?"

The wailing increases.

"Please, Mom. Tell me what's wrong."

I feel my blood pressure gradually rise. I pause. I force myself to speak slower, keep my voice low and look at her face.

"Mom, I'm here to help you. You seem frustrated and upset, and I don't blame you."

Amid the tears, her eyes seek mine.

"How aggravating it must be, Mom, not being able to tell me what you want to say."

I realize that I am aggravated, too, and that I have to calm myself before I can help her.

I take a deep breath, hold it for a few seconds, and slowly exhale. She continues to weep.

"Help me to understand. May I hold your hand, Mom?" Slowly she reaches out to meet my outstretched hand, and I remember how she used to reach out to comfort me when I was a little girl crying.

The sobbing starts to subside as my warm hand encircles hers. I stroke her hand gently. We both feel better.

Highlights:
When I am mindful and take a few slow, deep breaths, I relax and remember that touch can comfort when words fail.

STORY 37

Caught in the Middle

My teenage daughter rushes into the kitchen.

"Mom, it's eleven o'clock already. You promised me you'd take me shopping today."

"I know. I know. While you've been sleeping, I put up three loads of wash, straightened out the house and walked the dog. Saturday is my day off, too, you know," I sharply exclaim, totally harried.

"I am overwhelmed with all I have to do. And we have to see Grandpa today," I add, my face feeling flushed.

"Why bother, Mom? You know he doesn't even recognize you." "Or me," she mutters, under her breath.

"But Heather. Even if he doesn't remember my name or yours, his face lights up whenever he sees us. His eyes tell me that he knows, and I still can see the love radiating out. I know that we still can touch each other."

"Mom, it makes me squirm to see him. He's no longer my grandpa!"

"Heather. I know how you feel. I weep inside for my father. But, he still is Grandpa. Just like you keep changing as you grow up, he keeps changing because of Alzheimer's. That doesn't mean that he doesn't love you. He just can't show it in the old way. Now it's up to us to help him out. I just wish someone would help me out," I blurt.

"But Mom, whenever I offer to help, you always say, 'Oh, I can do it myself'. So why bother asking?"

Highlights:
Now is the time for me to learn how to accept help from others.

STORY 38

But He's Only 54 Years Old! Early Onset

I don't know what to do next; it all seems so unbearable. Getting the kids off to school, going to work, chauffeuring everyone around, and supervising homework. I can't believe I have to do all of this alone. I'm stuck paying all the bills, taking care of the lawn - these had always been his jobs. People this young aren't supposed to get Alzheimer's, and yet it has happened to my husband, 54 years old. Now I have to take care of him, the whole family and earn a living when he should be the one taking care of us. It just isn't fair.

I miss how we would talk about the children, decide which movie to see, and plan vacations. I miss him.

My kids are 13 and 15. They need both parents now more than ever, with all that temptation and academic and peer pressure. But the decisions and the burden fall on my shoulders.

By the time I take care of everyone else, there's nothing left of me.

And you say I should take care of myself? Exercise? Attend support groups? That's a laugh. Just how do you propose I do that? There's just no time.

Highlights:
Managing my family and my life is all I can do. I hope that one day I will figure out how to take care of myself.

STORY 39

The At-Home Spa

Tonight, I pamper myself. Every suggestion that I have read about how to make my mother more comfortable and relaxed I do for myself. That means: since she is fast asleep and before she starts to wake up in the middle of the night, I can create my own personal spa. Canyon Ranch, move over.

I enter the bathroom.

I lower the lights to the soft glow of strategically placed nightlights.

I fill the bath tub with the hottest of water that is tolerable and pour in drops of lavender oil. (I know how the aroma of lavender relaxes my mother, and now it's my turn.)

I put on a CD to soak my stress away to the strains of soft music.

I place a bath pillow under my neck as I sink into the water.

I wet a hand towel and place it over any part of me that the water doesn't cover.

I place slices of cool cucumber over my closed eyes as my body steeps in the hot, soothing water.

I sip a cup of chamomile tea with honey as I luxuriate in the warmth, and feel the tension melt, layer by layer.

I bask in the preciousness of this moment.

I enter a reverie of peace and serenity.

And when sated, I ever so slowly emerge to be refreshed as I re-connect with myself, body and soul.

Highlights:
I need to carve out some sacred time for me and create my at-home spa now.

STORY 40

I Just Can't Stand the Strain

It's the chronic anxiety. I cannot seem to escape it. Even when things are relatively peaceful, I am hyper vigilant, which makes me 'hyper'. My speech is pressured, my tone sharp, and my face constricted. I seem to have no control over it. I sense this because after an exhausting day, I have trouble falling asleep at night, and when I do, I wake up every two hours even though my husband is sleeping soundly beside me. Too many times, I awake in the middle of the night and see that he is gone. In a millisecond, I am out of bed, calling out his name, searching throughout the house, hoping he hasn't figured out how to open up the outside doors. My heart is racing. Perhaps I need to see a doctor.

My friends tell me to relax. They ask me, "What have you done for yourself lately?" I mumble some nonsense. I get annoyed. How can I take care of myself when the overriding priority is taking care of my husband?

In desperation, I sit down during his nap time and start to write. The experts call this 'journaling,' but for me, it's a way I can expel a little of the tension that builds up inside me.

Afterward, I feel some relief. I tell myself to close my eyes, breathe and savor the minute. I make myself slow down. The thoughts of dread that race through my head are now on paper, outside of me. For a moment, I am free. Then the anxiety returns.

Highlights:

I know that writing, or even just taking deep breaths, helps me to release some of the anxiety that I feel inside. But I have to face the facts: the anxiety never stops and it's time to talk to the doctor to see what else I can do to settle my nerves.

STORY 41

More Repetitions!

"Where is Jack?"

"Dad, Jack was here this morning. You and he just spoke together."

"No he wasn't. Where is Jack?"

"Dad, I just told you he was here this morning."

"Where is Jack?"

My brother Jack visits often but Dad just can't remember. As I begin to seethe I stop, remembering something I read. Then I say.

"Dad, Jack is on your mind, isn't he?"

"Why, yes."

"You wish he would stop by so you two can talk. Do you like talking to him?"

"All the time. He's still my little boy."

"Do you miss him?"

"Sure do."

"Well, the next time Jack stops by, I'm going to ask him to write it down here on your calendar so we can remember. He'll be back soon."

"When?"

"Tomorrow."

My father stops asking. Until the next time.

Highlights:
When I remember that one of the reasons why Dad repeats himself is because that person or subject is on his mind, I am better able to tolerate him.

STORY 42

'D' is for Depression

D is for Depression. That's the name of this day for me. And, I am Discouraged. There seems to be no end to the onerous task of overseeing the well-being of my father. My sister came out for an extended visit – one month – and I actually had a taste of my life again. Going out, being with my friends, and going to work without worrying about Dad. But now my sister has gone back to her home – 2000 miles away – and I am in worse shape than before she arrived. That taste of freedom undid me.

How can I handle all of this? My work suffers and I suffer. How long can I let my father stay home by himself? How do I figure this out?

I know that I am supposed to talk about this burden with others who understand, but I feel that all I do is complain. I know I'm supposed to contact the Alzheimer's Association - and I'm sure they have sources to help me -but making that phone call is so hard for me. I use all my energy to go to work and to reach out to my Dad. His continuing decline unnerves me. I can't believe that he keeps asking the same questions over and over again. It takes all my resolve not to yell back at him, "But, I just answered that!" I try to remember to explore what it is he is trying to say. I try to remember that he keeps repeating himself because he's probably anxious. I am frustrated and exhausted. Slowly I realize that, if I keep on going on like this, I'll collapse: mentally and physically.

Highlights:
My depression is a sign to take care of myself and get help. I am worth it.

STORY 43

Forgiveness

Forgiveness. What a concept. Never thought I would want to look at that. Yet, I need to forgive to cleanse my soul.

There are so many people I guess I should forgive that it's hard to know where to start.

Can I ever forgive my wife for getting Alzheimer's? It sure has destroyed any semblance of the plans for our retirement. This unexpected new full-time job is far more demanding than the one I left.

Can I forgive the doctor for the initial misdiagnosis and delay in the start of medications?

Can I forgive our friends for avoiding us now that the disease is progressing?

Can I forgive my son who claims he lives too far away to ever help out?

Can I ever forgive myself for resenting my wife and our situation?

I look at this list, knowing that more people and situations belong on it than I can think of. As I review it, I notice, 'I' appear in all of them. I start a second list:

I am the one who stopped reaching out to friends because I feel embarrassed by the disintegration of my wife's ability to talk and relate.

I am the one who never calls anyone to ask for help, let alone ask my son.

But my wife is the one who always did the social arrangements. Now it's me and I don't do a good job of it.

Then it occurs to me: I am only human, stumbling my way through this maze of caregiving in the disease called Alzheimer's, a disease over which I have no control.

Highlights:
I need to forgive myself first before I can hope to forgive others.

PART IV

New Directions: No Signposts

My head tells me
To move on,
My heart tells me
To stay.
My head tells me
I have done enough,
My heart tells me
Don't leave.
My head tells me
I will still be there for you,
My heart tells me
It is time for me to live fully at last.
I can do both.

Judith London 2012

STORY 44

Letting Go

Letting go. How can I let go of my husband, that wonderful, caring man I fell in love with 50 years ago? He has changed so much. The truth is that despite my brave face, despite my trying to enter his world to understand what he wants, I am suffering. The pain I feel, the grief I feel, seems unending. How hard it is to see parts of him disintegrate before my eyes. And I still love him.

What I have to do is let go of the man he once was. This takes a long time. Alzheimer's goes on and on and there is a lot of time for me to work this through.

Eventually, it sinks in. I can let go of the man that once was, but not the man that is. I now accept him for who he is today. Yes, it's taken me a long time to get to this place, continually adjusting every day. I realize that as of this moment, he still has:

- a sparkle in his eye, but not as bright
- a deep, resonating voice, which I truly cherish now that he speaks less often
- a warm hand that encircles mine
- an infectious smile that makes me smile.

Whatever tomorrow brings, I must go with the flow. I do not want to let go of him while he breathes and lives. Yes, it's painful to see how much of him has been lost. But I want to focus on the here and now of who he is today: very much alive, just different. And to move on even as I love him.

Highlights:
I'm holding on to my love, holding on to life, and letting go of what used to be.

STORY 45

In Sickness and in Health

I am in a tough situation, filled with tough feelings and facing a tough decision. It all started last week.

My husband, Jack, gradually has been getting worse. He no longer remembers where the bathroom is, so I put up photographs of a sink and commode for him to identify the correct door. His outbursts are escalating, from garbled talk to shouting rages, and I am beginning to feel afraid. Last week, as we sat opposite each other eating lunch, without warning, he rose from the table, picked up a knife, and began to wave it at me menacingly, screaming curses. I'm sure he would have stabbed me if the table hadn't been between us.

I stood up and said, "Stop!" but he wouldn't listen. His eyes looked glazed over, lost in a world of inner demons. I backed away slowly, still facing him, as he was trying to figure out how to go around the table. I reached for the phone, knowing the moment for a decision had arrived. I hastily dialed 911, darted out the front door, and waited for help.

I'm lucky. Two policemen arrived within minutes. We entered the house, my husband still ranting away. Jack dropped the knife and stopped yelling the moment he saw their uniforms. He looked bewildered. Gently but with authority, the police led him to the waiting ambulance where he was taken to the Emergency Room for evaluation.

The emergency room staff checked him for a bladder infection to see if delirium accounted for his bizarre behavior, but that wasn't the problem. I was told he was healthy physically and that this violent behavior was simply another twist in the way Alzheimer's affects some individuals.

They kept him for 72 hours, administered some medication, and Jack seemed to straighten out. The hospital released him into my care, and now as I drive home with him, I still feel apprehensive. Never before had I thought he would try to hurt me. I realize that I must prepare for this to happen again, and make a plan to prevent us both from harm.

After we arrive home and I settle him in, I pick up the phone to make an appointment with his neurologist for a re-evaluation. Afterward, I check my files and read papers that I had obtained from the Alzheimer's Association about how to go about placing someone in a residential memory care facility. I make some phone calls. I feel two minutes of relief because I am taking sensible actions.

Then the regrets and the guilt begin to set in. How could I even think of him leaving home? Why couldn't I just keep taking care of him 'in sickness and in health'? Whoever wrote those marriage vows never had to face Alzheimer's. I sigh. Out of necessity, I know that I must find a place that is safe - for him and for me - day and night. Then it hits me – he will no longer be at my side after I take that step.

> **Highlights:**
> I painfully realize that I must take steps to guarantee my safety and that of my husband. I am sad about what lies ahead.

STORY 46

Gibberish

The unthinkable is happening. Every time I think I have a handle on this disease, another unforeseeable problem emerges. Mom has started to talk gibberish.

I stop by to see my mother who's had Alzheimer's for the past three years. She seems to be doing well enough, managing with the family pitching in most days. I ask her,

"Mom, how are you doing today?" and she says,

"No-ky do-ky."

Now does that mean she's okay or not okay? My heart beat quickens. She is not using understandable words.

"Mom, are you okay?"

"No, of course," she says, looking surprised at my question.

"Mom, it's just that when you say something that sounds like 'no' in front of a 'yes', I get confused."

"I no fine speak," she replies, her voice louder than usual.

"Mom. I have a hard time knowing what you mean."
I struggle to regain my composure.

Highlights:
My heart breaks as I see her loss of coherent speech.
I will have to redouble my efforts to understand her
now.

STORY 47

The Crisis of Wandering Plus

My father wanders about the house half the night, something he's been doing regularly for the last eight weeks. This morning he wakes up at 10am. Although it is such a relief that at least he slept late, I am exhausted.

I'm glad I have that sensor device that awakens me at night whenever he leaves his room but then I get up, too. I found a way to secure the outside doors by installing those dead bolt locks. I remove the knobs of the stove after dinner so that I don't have to worry about him turning on the gas. Despite these precautions, my stomach churns every night.

I decide to call my brother who lives out-of-town. My brother really cares about me and Dad.

"James, Dad's wandering has me worried sick despite all the precautions we've taken."

"You've been putting up with this a long time."

I think about how I have tried to solve this night-time wandering problem. Not to mention the incontinence.

"We go outside every afternoon because sunlight is supposed to improve night-time sleep, but it's harder and harder for him to walk. I know I should try to sit outside with him in the late afternoon sun but he's so restless then. I limit his after-lunch nap to 45 minutes, but it's a struggle to waken him. I make sure he doesn't eat or drink after 7pm. I bring him to the toilet every two hours during the day but he still wets himself. And you remember what happened when we once tried sleeping pills."

"Yeah. You told me that he got up anyway after a few hours, and then was even more unsteady on his feet, unable to find the bathroom, and he sounded delirious."

"James - it just seems that nothing deters him from his middle-of-the-night prowl and those 'accidents'. A good daughter would hang in, I tell myself, but I know that I am starting to deteriorate."

"You are a good daughter. And a good sister, too. But, you cannot let the stress and lack of sleep make you sick. I don't want to see that. I've heard about what happens to caregivers like you. Too often the caregiver is the hidden victim and your physical and mental health breaks down. Meanwhile, the person you love that you've been caring for survives."

"I wish I could just keep going on anyway, James, but I see that Dad's not going to get better: Alzheimer's doesn't work that way."

"You know how grateful I am that you are there for Dad but Julie - maybe it's time to follow that plan we made for residential placement."

Months ago, my brother and I prepared what to do when Dad got worse.

We did our research then, my brother surfing the Web for memory care residences for my Dad in advance. I asked around, contacting some of those people who had been in my caregiver support group. When my brother visited four months ago, we got someone to stay with Dad so we could check out all the sites. We visited the local places to see which ones demonstrated a caring and respectful attitude toward their residents. We even had Dad come with us to see which one he liked when we had narrowed the list down to two places nearby.

"I know that's what we should do. But, I feel terrible about it." I sigh.

"Julie, I'm going to search through my papers for the guidelines we got from the Alzheimer's Association to see what they say about transition to a nursing home," James added, quietly.

With very mixed feelings, deep inside we both know that this is the right thing to do. But it is so painful.

Highlights:
Night-time wandering and incontinence wear me down. I feel awful about placing Dad in a memory care residence, but maybe it's time.

STORY 48

A Tough Conversation

My sister, my brother and I finally come to a decision. We are going ahead with our plan to place Dad in a memory care residence. What do we say to Dad? How do we approach this? We are torn up about what we have to do.

We turn to the Alzheimer's Association guidelines for direction. My brother and my sister and I talk at length, and write out what we want to say to Dad. I am the designated spokesperson because I've been the main caregiver for years. My brother and sister pitch in.

We decide to sit down together with Dad in my living room.

"Daddy, I am feeling so run down lately and the doctor said I need to take a rest."

My father shifts his glance from the floor to us.

"Yes, I asked Bill and Joan to be here because they care so much about you and me."

He looks at me.

"Dad, we found an opening at the place that you and I visited a while ago. You liked it.

It was the place that had a great piano player and we all sang *You Are My Sunshine* together."

He begins to sing, "You are my sunshine," and we join in.

"Yes Dad. We have so much fun singing together. You'll stay there for a while."

"I want to stay here."

"I know you do, Dad. I wish you could, too, 'cause I've gotten used to you living with me. But we have to try it out."

"I stay here."

"Dad I know you want to. But Bill or Joan or I will visit you every day to add even more sunshine. We'll always be there for you. We love you."

"That nice lady?"

"Oh – you mean Linda, the lady who helps us out?"

"Yes, Linda."

"Linda has her family to think of, Dad, and they miss her."

"Oh."

"There'll be more people like Linda in the new place."

My Dad sighs and folds his arms. Unconvinced.

Highlights:

This conversation is so painful. Reluctantly, we come to the conclusion that moving to a memory care residence is the best thing for our father and for me. But it hurts.

STORY 49

Forgiving Ourselves About Placement

The deed is done. I placed my mother in a memory care residential unit. But instead of feeling relief, relief that I can now sleep at night without worrying about her wandering around the house or sneaking outside for a walk in the middle of the night, I am filled with guilt. Lucky for me, I am meeting with my best friend today.

After we hug and say hello, I blurt out,

"What could I have done differently to keep my mother at home longer? I've put her in a nursing home! I think to myself, I never should have done that."

"Oh, Jane."

"I never should have gone out for coffee with my friends when she was taking that predictable nap after lunch. When I got back, I found her frantically calling out my name, looking for me, and darting around from room to room."

"Jane, wait a minute..."

But I can't stop spitting out a litany of mistakes now that I've started.

"I never should have fallen asleep that night she wandered out of the house. Luckily, I awoke to discover that the front door was wide open and she was already at the curb. I never should have…"

I list one slip-up after another. Finally she interrupts me, exclaiming,

"STOP! Stop beating yourself up! Stop throwing darts at yourself. It is bad enough that Alzheimer's has attacked your mother. Don't let it demolish you!"

Highlights:
When the voice of compassion cannot come from within me, I need to listen to the compassionate words of those who understand what I am going through.

STORY 50

Just in Time

At a meeting of our caregiver support group, I say to a new member, "I almost waited too long."

"What do you mean?"

"Well, my dear wife of 55 years has been the center of my life for so long - and in the last few years with Alzheimer's, taking care of her had become my whole life. I wasn't paying much attention to myself until one morning I awoke and noticed that my left arm ached, and I thought that I had slept in an awkward position. The pain persisted and then radiated up my arm toward my shoulder, and my chest felt tight. I realized that maybe I was having a heart attack. I dialed my daughter who lives nearby, because someone had to stay with my wife. Then I dialed 911."

"What was going on?'

"I am very lucky. It turns out that I had a mild heart attack, and that was some wake-up call. But that day, my first thoughts had been: *how will my wife get along*, not *dial 911 immediately*."

"That's what happens to us, doesn't it? We come last."

"My daughter came right over before the ambulance arrived. I probably would have kept on waiting if she hadn't gotten there so quickly. When I got home from the hospital a few days later, I met with my kids, who finally understood what I've been going through. They began the search for memory care residences for us to check out. I had been avoiding that issue for many months even though I knew my wife was getting worse. Fortunately, we heard about a place that had rave reviews for the loving care and stimulating activities they provide their residents."

"And?"

"Well we visited that one and it looked like a great spot for my wife. Then I wondered: how can she get along without me? How can I get along without her? Will they take good care of her? Will we be happy?" And, I had to face the harsh reality that I must take care of myself, too."

"What did you do?"

"We made the decision to go ahead and move her in as soon as possible so that I could get well."

"How did you tell your wife about it?"

"Actually, I'm so glad it worked out. Three weeks ago, my daughter brought her over to the residence, telling her that I was away for out-of-town medical tests, and that she needed to stay at this new place while I was gone. Sweetheart that she still is, she went along willingly. Of course a few days before, we had brought over her favorite clothes, lots of family photographs, her favorite quilt and bedspread, and anything else we could think of, so that the room would look familiar."

"I have heard that you can include your loved one in the transition by bringing her to the new place for lunch or having her join some activities even before you make the move," the leader interjected and continued,

"The important thing is to find a way that works for you and your family, and that minimizes stress for everyone involved."

"Thanks for saying that. Our way worked for us. And the amazing thing is that I visit my wife several times a week, and she seems so happy. She thinks she is in a hotel – and the staff treats her so kindly and cares for her even better that I could."

"How do you feel now that it seems to be working out?"

"You know, I still feel a little guilty when I wake up in the morning and notice I slept until 8:30 am. I no longer jump out of bed with a start thinking, - oh no – where is she - is she alright? Instead, as I get out of bed, I say to myself that she is safe, and I am liberated - free to do whatever I choose to do. I look forward to visiting my wife each day because I want to, not because I have to. And I can get on with my life."

Highlights:

I am lucky that I found a good memory care residence for my wife even though it took my own health problems to recognize what I had to do. It works better for both of us.

STORY 51

More Decisions:
A Feeding Tube?

As I prepare dinner, the phone rings. I jump with a start.

"Ginny, it's me." I recognize my sister Grace's voice.

"Oh, hi Grace. What's up?"

"I stopped by the nursing home to see Mom and she still won't eat, even when I encourage her and make the motions of eating. The nurses tell me that the doctor wants us to okay the insertion of a feeding tube!"

"Oh, no. Mom would hate that!"

"I know. It's terrible."

I feel tears welling up in my own eyes and despair settling in. As I have had to do so often in the past, I take a deep breath.

"Oh, Grace. We can't let that happen. We've got to talk about it. Stop by and have dinner here on your way home so we can figure out what to do."

"Okay."

When Grace arrives, I breathlessly begin to speak even before she takes off her coat.

"While I was waiting for you, I found my copy of Mom's Advanced Directives. Grace, Mom was clear: no feeding tubes."

"Oh. Somehow, that had slipped my mind. You know, that's odd: the people at the nursing home didn't refer to those papers either."

"Look how hard it is for us to remember," I say, and I begin to serve dinner.

"I know it's silly but suddenly I'm thinking about how much Mom would love this pot roast. It was her favorite."

"I know. I followed her recipe."

"Remember how she adored chocolate ice cream, night after night?"

"And savored every mouthful." We smile as we ache, and then put down our forks, no longer feeling like eating anymore.

"Ginny, you know that no matter how hard we try, she just won't eat now."

"Could she just be sick with something else?"

"The staff checked her out and she isn't sick."

"Mom would be furious with us if she thought that we weren't honoring her wishes."

"I know but I dread telling the doctor and the nurses: no feeding tube. They'll think we are cruel and no longer care whether or not she lives. The way they looked at me when I didn't agree to that tube insertion this afternoon – like I was a murderer or something."

"Now that we have to face this, it's so hard to respect what Mom wanted us to do."

"Yes, but she trusted us, Ginny."

"I know." Stumbling over the words I say,

"We'll just have to tell the doctor: no feeding tube. We must follow Mom's wishes."

"But are we doing the right thing, Ginny? Insisting that she not be given the nourishment she needs to live?"

"We have to. It's not about how we feel but what Mom wanted."

Then we get up from the table, and give each other a long, tearful hug.

> **Highlights:**
> I must respect my mother's wishes: no feeding tubes. I am doing the right thing even though I dread the outcome.

STORY 52

Nothing to Talk About

Now that my father is in a nursing home, we have nothing to talk about. Uneasiness tempers my new-found relief.

When I visit him, he seems to have no recollection of his grandson who is a star high school baseball player. We used to go to all the games together, my Dad cheering my boy on. He never asks about him now. Does that ever hurt. He doesn't remember his grandson.

I bring this up in my support group for relatives of those with Alzheimer's. Other people share similar stories. Then one woman whose husband has been in the residence for over six months tells us how she relates to her husband.

"He never brings up anything on his own. I have to talk about subjects that used to mean something to him and that gets him started. No matter what he says, I agree and smile a lot. Perhaps you need to start the ball rolling and talk to your Dad about your son and baseball. Maybe even bring your son in to visit him."

"I never thought of that. I've been focusing on how indifferent he is and protecting my son. I take it personally. But you're saying that it's the disease that stops him and that I have to take the ball and run with it."

Highlights:
Although I feel sad for my father, for myself, and for my son who will never see his grandpa the way he used to be, I realize that I need to start conversations with my Dad based on topics that used to be important to him.

STORY 53

Romance

I meet my friend, Julie, for coffee, not quite sure about what I will say. After we greet one another, I take a deep breath, and begin.

"I was at the memory care residence to see my Stan, my husband, like I do practically every day. I check his room but he's not there. I look into the dining room and blink twice. Stan is sitting there holding the hand of Sophie, another resident."

Silence. Finally, Julie says,

"Wow. If that happened to me, I'd be upset."

I continue,

"I know. I am in shock. Confused. Jealous. Indignant. I control myself. I go over to them and greet Stan a little uncertainly. He stands up grinning and says hello."

"At least he still knows it's you," Julie says.

"'Hi Honey,' I manage to say, 'I see you have a new friend,' swallowing my emotions.

'Oh.'

'Would you like to come with me to catch up on what's going on?'

'OK'

"'Excuse us, Sophie, Stan will be back to see you later,' I manage to say."

"And off we go back to his room where we sit down and he reaches for my hand, as if nothing had happened. I am hurt and puzzled."

"Did you talk to him about it?"

"No. I stick with the usual stuff – ask him how he is, tell him about the grandkids. He seems to enjoy hearing about them and shakes his head, looking proud. After an hour or so, I get up to leave, and he kisses me goodbye."

"You mean you didn't say anything at all about it?"

"By that time, I thought, what's the point? He lives in the present moment, and doesn't remember what just happened, so why upset him? When I get home, I put my feelings aside. I think that even though I have always been there for him throughout our 53 years of marriage, he needs to relate to someone when I am not around. And you know what? I surprise myself by gradually feeling happy that he has found someone there, even if it is another woman. And, he chose a real pretty lady, too."

Highlights:
I never would have thought that my husband would find romance with someone else, and that I'd even come to see the positive side of it. I am learning so much about myself and my capacity to move on.

STORY 54

Now What? Starting Over

Today I face the first day that my husband is not by my side. How empty I feel. I don't know what to do with myself except to get dressed, have my breakfast and run over to the nursing home where he now resides. Doesn't that defeat the reason why we placed him there in the first place?

My kids were so worried about me, how I've aged in the last four years of caring for him. How isolated I have become. It looks like both he and I were succumbing to this disease. I know that placing him is an act of survival for me as well as for him, but what am I supposed to do now?

I ask myself, where was I, 58 years ago when we first got married, and four years ago when Alzheimer's descended upon us? Here I am, 80 years old and I feel like a beginner in this journey of life. After spending all this time desperately trying to reconnect with him, how do I reconnect with myself?

I make myself breakfast and sit down to read the morning newspaper. I look across the table where he used to sit. I go back to reading about the ills of the world, trying to lose myself in everyone else's problems. I get involved in a few articles, and when I look at my watch before getting up to pour myself another cup of coffee, I am surprised to see that 15 minutes passed by. Good. I can do this, one moment at a time.

Highlights:
I can <u>be</u> with my own feelings – no matter what they are – and honor this process of change in my life.

PART V

Help For Unsung Heroes

THE LISTENER

My dearest, what are you saying?
I try to understand your words.
Your voice goes up and down,
Sounding earnest then annoyed.
I nod my head
Not knowing if you know
I nod my head from desperation, not understanding,
To keep our connection alive
though the thread between us is frayed,
I nod my head because I love you.

Judith London 2012

Summary of Highlights

1. I am worried. What does this change in behavior mean? Is it depression, infection or a form of dementia? I better call the doctor now.
2. I cannot permit someone else's denial of the truth make me doubt what I know.
3. I need to keep on reporting the facts, whether or not anyone else understands. The important thing is that I understand.
4. I can't believe how sensible my mother is after hearing this diagnosis of Alzheimer's. If only I could be as wise as she is.
5. My support group helps me see that variations in intelligibility *are* part of Alzheimer's, and that my confusion is valid.
6. Letting someone like my Mom remain an independent driver for as long as possible can be nerve-wracking as I check up on her driving ability. I hope I can learn to enjoy the ride!
7. I can keep on socializing despite this disease. My friends may be more understanding than I could ever imagine.
8. What a realization! Repeating jokes can be another way to maintain a loving connection. Instead of groaning inside, I'm going to laugh along with him.
9. Some changes can be unexpectedly lovely if I let go of the past.
10. I am the one who can think straight. I must make sound decisions, even if it means overruling my mother.
11. Alzheimer's has changed my mother into the mother I always wanted.

12. It is exhausting when I have to figure out the meaning of his repeated words and behavior. But when I stop and try to understand, we connect.
13. I feel such an ache whenever I recall the 'good old days'. It's hard to accept him as he is today.
14. Like the hummingbird, I will have faith that our love remains steady amid the ups and downs of this disease.
15. Music can bypass the conscious brain and contact the heart to help me and my soul mate connect. I cherish these moments.
16. I am learning to make peace with the changes that keep on happening to us, and treasure the moments we have together.
17. By taking some simple precautions to protect someone who wanders, I can breathe a sigh of relief.
18. Once you get him started, he may still know how to do something he could do years before. What a thrill.
19. Sometimes I just have to laugh and know that I forget, too.
20. I am amazed that cookies and milk work wonders for my mid-night wanderer. And, to think that snoring would reassure me that all is well.
21. I know Mom may become angry or insulted, but I need to make sure she no longer drives now that I see she has lost the ability to be aware of her limitations.
22. When I focus on things she still can do, we both feel better. And I can learn what I, eventually, will have to do.
23. When something I do awakens his memory, it is a victory over Alzheimer's.

24. I miss my wife, who, for so long, had been my equal partner. But I tell myself to acknowledge her as she is today, and savor the moment.

25. When I can see the humor in a trying situation, it relieves the tension.

26. My kids may be young, but they do have the ability to connect with my Dad. When they visit their grandfather, unexpected moments of delight may unfold.

27. When I re-create a situation at home that Mom used to love and she responds I feel close to her.

28. It may take me a while but I finally remember to stop, look and listen to my Dad. Then I realize: his actions speak louder than the words he cannot say.

29. With a reminder from the past, we can still share magical moments amid all the pain and longing.

30. I won't wait until it's my birthday. I will ask for my present early: someone to relieve me.

31. I need to forgive myself for being so impatient and angry. I realize that once I lead the way and initiate what needs to be done, my husband follows what I do. For now.

32. When I overcome my resistance to asking for help, I find people more willing to help out than I thought.

33. Whether Dad is upset or OK, I realize that I must reach out for help and make time just for me.

34. We are all simply human with human limitations. I can have compassion for my father *and* I can have compassion for myself as well.

35. Like it or not, I need to share what I'm going through. Despite my discomfort about speaking up.

36. When I am mindful and take a few slow, deep breaths, I relax and remember that touch can comfort when words fail.

37. Now is the time for me to learn how to accept help from others.

38. Managing my family and my life is all I can do. I hope that one day, I will figure out how to take care of myself.

39. I will carve out some sacred time for me and create my at-home spa now.

40. I know that writing, or even just taking deep breaths, helps me to release some of the anxiety that I feel inside. But I have to face the facts: the anxiety never stops and it's time to talk to the doctor to see what else I can do to settle my nerves.

41. When I remember that one of the reasons why Dad repeats himself is because that person or subject is on his mind, I am better able to tolerate him.

42. My depression is a sign to take care of myself and get help. I am worth it.

43. I need to forgive myself first before I can hope to forgive others.

44. I'm holding on to my love, holding on to life, and letting go of what used to be.

45. I painfully realize that I must take steps to guarantee my safety and that of my husband. I am sad about what lies ahead.

46. My heart breaks as I see her loss of coherent speech. I will have to redouble my efforts to understand her now.

47. Night-time wandering and incontinence wear me down. I feel awful about placing Dad in a memory care residence, but maybe it's time.

48. This conversation is so painful. Reluctantly, we come to the conclusion that placing Dad in a memory care residence is the best thing for our father and for me. But it hurts.

49. When the voice of compassion cannot come from within me, I need to listen to the compassionate words of those who understand what I am going through.

50. I am lucky that I found a good memory care residence for my wife even though it took my own health problems to recognize what I had to do. It works better for both of us.

51. I must respect my mother's wishes: no feeding tubes. I am doing the right thing even though I dread the outcome.

52. Although I feel sad for my father, for myself, and for my son who will never see his Grandpa the way he used to be, I realize that I have to start conversations with my Dad based on topics that used to be important to him.

53. I never would have thought that my husband would find romance with someone else, and that I'd be able to see the positive side of it. I am learning so much about myself and my capacity to move on.

54. I can be with my own feelings – no matter what they are – and honor this process of change in my life.

Key Terms

Caregiver: someone who has the principal responsibility for caring for another who needs help.

Dementia: a set of symptoms that affects how a person functions day-to-day. It includes memory loss, plus impairment in judgment, intellect or language. One may picture **dementia as an overall umbrella**, with one or more of the following types falling underneath it:

1. **Alzheimer's**, a disease of the brain that accounts for approximately **70%** of dementia, characterized by:
   - Gradual onset with a steady slow irreversible progression.
   - Confusion, disorientation, language difficulties, forgetfulness, and problems figuring out how to get from one place to another.
   - Decline in ability to learn new information on a conscious level. However, **unconscious memory still exists** so that a person with dementia may still be able to pick up impressions without knowing why.
   - Debris in the brain that clumps together to interfere with one cell communicating with another, eventually leading to disintegration of the brain cell or neuron.
   - The gradual destruction progresses to affect every area of life until all systems fail over time.

2. **Vascular dementia**: accounts for about **20%** of dementia. It relates to a problem with the blood flow to or in the brain. It occurs suddenly, typically as a stroke. Memory deficits

occur with respect to the area of the brain affected and impaired memory may remain stable unless another stroke or brain illness occurs.

3. **Lewy body dementia**: typified by unusual clusters of a protein that accumulate in one area of the brain, symptoms frequently start with tremors, unsteadiness, delusions or hallucinations, as well as increasing memory loss. When Lewy bodies are scattered throughout the brain without memory loss, it is called Parkinson's disease.

4. **Frontotemporal dementia**: evidenced by damage to cells in the front and sides of the brain. Personality changes, disinhibition, compulsions, and apathy usually precede memory loss.

5. **Dementia from Head Injury** or other neurological illness, as well as **alcoholism**.

6. **Mixed dementia**: a situation where more than one type of dementia coexists with another. Once the brain has been weakened with one brain ailment, it becomes more vulnerable to additional kinds of dementia.

7. **Mild Cognitive Impairment** (MCI) refers to excessive memory loss, but with the individual still able to function. Each year approximately 12% of those with MCI convert to Alzheimer's. Over a four year period, about 50% convert to Alzheimer's.

Memory Loss:

- **Immediate memory** loss is not being able to recall what was said or happened a few seconds ago. People with Alzheimer's remember 'only in the moment'.

- **Short-term memory loss** is forgetting what happened recently. For example, someone may forget that he just had breakfast, or cannot recall that he saw his son the day before. It occurs early in Alzheimer's and other dementias.
- **Long-term memory** loss is forgetting what happened a long time ago. This occurs in later stages of Alzheimer's and other dementias.

A Baker's Dozen on How to Take Care of Yourself

1. Avoid isolation: talk to someone who understands.
2. Join a support group in person.
3. Have your loved one with Alzheimer's attend a support group.
4. Look into adult day care centers for your loved one.
5. Can't get out? Go to an on-line or telephone chat room.
6. Breathe deeply.
7. Take a walk.
8. Get some exercise.
9. Arrange a coffee or luncheon date with a friend.
10. Ask for help from family, friends, and any group you belong to.
11. Laugh a lot.
12. Meditate.
13. Treat yourself to spa care – maybe a massage!

Write down at least one nurturing thing you commit to doing for only *you*.

Guide to Dominant Themes

Theme	Story Number
Acceptance	4, 16, 24, 44
Change	9, 11, 16, 22, 24, 54
Compassion	34, 49
Connection	8, 9, 15, 18, 26, 27, 29, 36
Courage	A Salute to Unsung Heroes – p. 155
Decisions	1, 6, 21, 45, 49, 51
Denial	2, 3, 10
Disbelief	1, 4, 11
Driving	6, 21
Exhaustion	30, 33, 35, 37, 38, 40, 47
Fear	45
Finances	32
Forgiveness	31, 43, 49
Frustration	3, 28, 31, 33, 35, 46
Grief	13, 46, 51
Humor	19, 20, 25
Lonely	13, 54
Love	14, 15, 23, 27, 29, 44, 53
Placement	45, 47, 48, 49, 50
Relief	17, 50
Repetition	8, 12, 41
Sadness	35, 42, 46, 48, 51

Guide to Dominant Themes continued

A Few Resources for Caregivers

Alzheimer's Association. www.alz.org 1-800-272-3900.

All-inclusive information about every aspect of dementia. Caregiver chat room.

Division of Motor Vehicles. www.dmv.gov

Section on Senior Drivers outlines policy in your respective state.

London, Judith L. 2009. *Connecting the Dots: Breakthroughs in Communication as Alzheimer's Advances.* Oakland, CA: New Harbinger Publications.

Tools to reach out to connect and communicate plus relevant information.

Sharecare.com. www.sharecare.com.

Click on 'Brain,' then type in 'Alzheimer's.' Ask any question and an expert will answer.

WebMd. www.exchanges.webmd.com/alzheimers-exchange.

Alzheimer's Community consisting of caregivers, and some people who have Alzheimer's, to exchange information and provide support. Currently, Dr. London is the Alzheimer's expert for the site.

A Salute to Unsung Heroes

It takes courage to take care of someone with Alzheimer's or another dementia.

It takes courage to face the seeming endlessness of it all.

Where do we find the strength to do this?

For some of us, it is love: the love that we have for this person who has Alzheimer's or another dementia: the long-time love that sustains us regardless of what happens.

For some of us, it is an obligation: an obligation to show up because we are supposed to show up, regardless of the way we feel.

For some of us, it is a paid job, one that serves others in their time of need.

For some of us, it is remembering: remembering how this person used to be there for us, so now is the time we must be there for him or her.

For some of us, it is a belief that a Higher Power will get us through these troubled times, that a Higher Power will guide us through the journey.

For some of us, it is the belief that the human spirit will survive the onslaught of this disease and that this is true for us as well as our loved one with Alzheimer's.

It may be hard for a person with Alzheimer's to appreciate what we are doing.

It may be hard for someone with Alzheimer's to say 'thank you," especially when saying "thank you" has always been a hard thing to say.

Make no mistake about it: you have courage. Bravo.

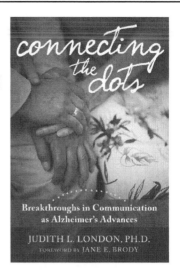

Made in the USA
Lexington, KY
24 March 2014